The Darkness of His Dreams

Poetry

John W. Leys

Broken Wing Publishing
Redmond, Oregon

All the poems in this book were, in some form, originally published on the blog Darkness of His Dreams (darknessofhisdreams.wordpress.com), except for:

'Blood Into Ink,' which was originally published on the blog Blood Into Ink (https://bloodintoinkpressblog.wordpress.com/).

Cover Photo by Justine K. Leys
Cover Design by John W. Leys

ISBN: 978-1-7333645-0-8 (Paperback)
ISBN: 978-1-7333645-1-5 (eBook)

Library of Congress Control Number:2019910522

First Published August 2019 by Broken Wing Publishing

Dedicated to
Karen Sue Leys (1952-2018)

My Mom. My first fan.
She always supported and encouraged me in whatever I did.
I miss her more than I can say.

"To gain your own voice, forget about having it heard.

— Allen Ginsberg

Contents

ACKNOWLEDGMENTS   72

ABOUT THE AUTHOR   75

The Darkness of His Dreams

Songs of the Soul

Songs of love and death,
Innocence and experience,
Writ on water and leaves of grass,
Sing the song of deliverance

Lyrics flow a bubbling brook
Howling in the canyons of Cain.
Pleasure flows, rain explodes
Verses sooth like a cool spring rain.

The Darkness of His Dreams

Disfigured by a clubfootedness of the heart
No visible limp or gait
No sign to alert parent or peer
To the barely bearable weight

Achieving as much or more
With seemingly little effort
A heart strains under expectations weight
Praying from this earth to be severed.

Love weighs as much as hatred
Sometimes even more-so
Surrounded by family and friends
Isolated and lonesome as Caruso

They all want a hero
Not an uncommon want, it seems
But in whom does a hero confide
The true darkness of his dreams?

Laying Awake in the Darkness

I've felt old and ancient
Since I was 12 years old,
Worn out, road weary,
For reasons unexplained
Living in the Cleaver household
In an idyllic isolated Oregon valley.
It made me want to believe in reincarnation,
The only explanation for the
Spread thin butter feeling
That started in the 3rd grade
When I reasoned out
That death meant oblivion
Not fluffy clouds and angels,
Training myself not to think of it,
To fend off the icy black hole
Opening under my sternum,
Crushing everything within its event horizon.
I lay in bed, tears streaming cheeks,
meaninglessness pressing down; suffocating
I start to scream,
Pretending to have had a nightmare,
So my mother will come, hold, and console.
Unable to articulate the existential crisis
Of an 8 year old boy.

Blood into Ink

Blood is too thick to write with
When you tear open a vein
With a fountain pen
To fill an empty India ink bottle--
Coagulation in the ink well,
Blood clots smeared across the page--
Dilute with salty tears,
Cried alone in the dark.
Your pen will run smooth
Across the page,
Cauterizing the wounds.

My Generation

I wasn't born with a club foot
I didn't fight in Vietnam
I didn't teach at Columbia
I wasn't fooled by Nixon's charms

My generation was as lost as Hemingway's
And just as productive.

I didn't escape Minnesota in a snowstorm,
I didn't go mad at Arfderydd
I didn't smash a guitar at Woodstock
I didn't drown in Delacroix

My generation was just as angry as Townshend's
And just as destructive.

Note: *Arfderydd (Welsh) is pronounced Arf-der-ith ("th" as in father) and is usually equated with modern day Arthuret in Cumbria, England.*

How it Started - *a pantoum*
For Justine

It all started with a photograph
A sample and a lure
Beauty captured in mid-laugh
A potion without a cure

A sample and a lure
A promise of things to come
A potion without a cure
A city without a slum

A promise of things to come
A prophecy self-fulfilled
A city without a slum
A foundation on which to build

A prophecy self-fulfilled
Beauty captured in mid-laugh
A foundation on which to build
It all started with a photograph

Still on the Road

Driving down the poison highway
Through the nightmares of my youth:
Saccharine poetry, suicidal thoughts;
Disastrous experiments with vermouth.

Sterilizing self-inflicted wounds
With tequila, scotch and beer.
Bathed in sticky sweat,
Self-loathing, and fear.

Decades down a dusty highway
Through the terrors of middle-age:
Thinning hair; graying beard
Covering the still smoldering rage.

Calming the demons of the mind
With a single chilled glass of mead,
Wounds healed; scars run deep,
And occasionally still bleed.

Seeking release from suffering
In Athens; under an old fig tree.
A chance to finally flourish,
Living life in true equanimity.

How Does it Feel?

*In answer to the question "How does it feel when your muse
runs his fingers through your hair, resting his palms bare on
your crown?"*

Its like being possessed by an effeminately androgynous angel,
who may not have fallen, but definitely has some explaining to do,
As words and visions pass through my brain, down my arm, and into
my right hand,
As if whispered in my ear by a one-eyed raven sitting on my shoulder
Telling me about his day.

There's a shot of adrenaline to my heart, pupils dilate,
And my hand is compulsed to write everything down,
Sensical or nonsensical, until the episode passes.
My cramping clenched fist tries hard to write legibly,
As the words come faster than I can safely write,
Pain surging arthritically through my bones.

In the end I'm left alone, in a post-coital haze,
To finish and polish the lunatical ravings
Scribbled in my little black notebook.

Is There Anybody Out There?

Can anyone out in the hallway hear me?
Skrit-Scratching on the walls,
Floor to ceiling pencil poems
In prescription-cursive fonts,
Hand cramps trying to keep up
With the torrent through my cortex.
Thoughts crying out, screaming the night,
Jolting awake, dream-fog questioning
The reality of sounds in the dark.
Strain to hear soft sobs through
Shared bathroom walls,
Fetal-curled on the tile floor.

Randomly reciting passages from Plato
Epictetus and the Buddha.
Waiting for the appropriate countersign
From Aristotle, Epicurus and the Gita.
Murmur-chanting *Howl* and *America*
Softly, steadily swaying like a Rabbi praying Torah.

Desperately shoving notes and folded photographs
Under the cell door, hoping an Orderly doesn't see.

Walls full, pencil broken
Poetry flows on, scratched into the floor,
A spiraling binding protection circle of words
Writ with a broken bloodied fingernail.

Tell Me What I Need to Know

Throne of gold up on high
The Ancient of Days sits,
Appearing like a Son of Adam,
White woolly whiskers
Uncombed hair and dirty feet.

Winged creatures come and go,
Speaking to Him of the world below,
Thought, Memory, raven, crow,
Come tell me what I need to know

> *Noah sent a raven out from the Ark to find dry land;*
> *There was none to be found, the rains washed it all away.*
> *He fed on the rotting floating corps of an iron smelter,*
> *Shat out an island for the dove to find and pissed a river.*
> *At least that's the story I heard from Utnapishtim's raven*
> *—I think his name was Neil—*
> *In a dream, while he dined on the rotted remains of a friend.*

Ancient All-father Asgard King,
One-eyed wandering Woden,
God of poets, inspiration and berserker rages,
Riding eight-legged Sleipner across the rainbow,
A raven on either shoulder, whispering in his ears.

At dawn they fly away and go,
At dinner they report on the world below,
Thought, Memory, raven, crow,
Tell me what I need to know.

The 道 of λόγος

The logos that can be defined
is not the one eternal Logos,
The word that can be spoken
is not the one true Word,
The tao that can be explained
is not the one everlasting Tao,
The force that can be described
is not the one indivisible Force,
The path that can be walked
is not the one true Path.

Known without learning,
Understood without knowing,
Arrived at without traveling.

One unified whole,
No sides to join,
No inside to be on the outside of,
All is one, one is all,
Forever momentary,
All pervasive,
Binding itself to itself.

Source of everything,
Bookend of eternity,
Rational structure of existence,
Unobtainable goal
That has already been reached.

Note: *λόγος (Greek, pronounced lógos) means "word," "speech," or "reason." A term often used in Hellenistic philosophy and Christian theology.* 道 *is the Tao of Taoism*

Wholeness

Not opposite
Poles apart,
Nor contradictions:
Complementary continuums,
Spectrums growing from
And into one another.

There is no tall
Without something short
To be taller than,
Nothing is close
Without something far
To be closer than,
Nothing dark
Without a light
To be darker than,
No light
Without a shadow,
No up
Without a down
To be upward from,
No left
Without a right
To be to the left of.

The stairs that lead up
Also lead down,
The road that goes away
Will also bring you back again.

Heraclitus' River - *a tanka*

The river flows on,
Ever changing; transforming,
Never stepped in twice:
Its never the same river,
And you're never the same man.

I Dreamed I Saw Old Socrates

I dreamed I saw old Socrates
Walking Athens after dark.
No people to harass, no questions to ask,
No great debates on which to embark.

His face it looked so serene,
As he contemplated truth.
Is this the man they put to death
For corruption of the youth?

The men in charge, to keep their jobs,
Don't want us thinking for ourselves.
Its sheep they need, easier to lead,
Not the depth to which wisdom delves.

Question every single authority,
Be certain only of what you do not know.
These men of Athens knew right then
This gadfly had to go.

I dreamed I saw old Socrates
Teaching with his last breath.
I stood among his crowd of friends
As he bravely met his death.

I awoke in tears of anger
At this injustice that had been done.
But I could not define what "justice" was,
And I knew that old Socrates had won.

That Dog Diogenes

I saw that dog Diogenes
Walking daylight, lamp in hand.
Wandering the streets of Athens,
Looking for one good man.

Living virtue naturally,
In a simple cloak he'd be dressed,
Indifferent to wealth or power,
By which the ignorant are so impressed.

Men, they complicate everything
With their customs and their laws.
Only wisdom and rationality can
Avoid the suffering these things cause.

Live your life in simplicity,
Want only what you truly need.
Your true self will start to flourish
Once unquenchable desire you cease to feed.

I saw Diogenes last Sunday,
Masturbating in the street,
"If only twas so easy," he said,
"To cure hunger without having to eat."

Humble lentils fill a belly,
Wine barrels provide a dry bed,
Collect all the gold your heart desires,
You'll still end your life dead.

Alexander saw Diogenes
Sunbathing by himself in Crete.
The great king saw within him
Not one ounce of evil or deceit.

Standing in awe of true wisdom,
Wanting to do what was right,
The king asked what wish he could grant him,
Diogenes said, "Get out of my fucking light!"

Exile and Enlightenment – a sonnet

A deserted beach, shipwreck on the shore,
Desolate remains of a life once shared,
Before it was clear what fate had in store
In Eden with you when our hearts were bared,

Forbidden fruit can ne'er be un-eaten
Once taught, good and evil can't be un-learned
Battles can't be won once you've been beaten,
Bridges can't be crossed once they've all been burned.

Alone we walk the paths on which we're hurled
Exiled to wilderness, where truth is found
To become ourselves, to create our world,
To accept the fate to which we are bound.

No way to be that you're not meant to be
No way to accept this and not be free

Quiet Desperation

Quiet desperation
Pressing down
Weighing on shoulders
Spirit cramping, muscle crushing
Promises of rewards
That may never come.

Working to survive,
Not to flourish,
Working for a future
You may not live to see.
Earn money to buy things
You were told could fill the voids.

Kept too busy by bourgeoisie billionaire banker masters
To even think.
For yourself,
About yourself,
To know what happiness truly is,
And what it requires.

Into the Woods

For Henry David Thoreau

Live life deliberately,
Minute by minute
Day by day,
Mindful of every moment
From birth to ultimate decay.

Don't be distracted
By trivialities, luxuries;
Empty goals for which the desperate strive,
And realize at the graveyard gate
That you were never truly alive.

Memento Mori – *a sonnet*

Went down the desert where the vultures feed
On human flesh rotting in the sunshine.
Pluck eyes, testicles, suck out the seed.
Bloated remains, corpses, on which they dine.

Bereft of life, we all end up a meal
For buzzards, for jackals, microbes and worms.
Most don't want to admit that death is real,
Its a truth with which all must come to terms.

If you live like you'll last a thousand years
The time to be a good man will ne'er come.
You'll end your life with your soul in arrears,
Fighting the fate you can ne'er escape from.

Slaves to fear and death are ne'er truly free,
Socrates didn't fear death, why should we?

For Vincent van Gogh

Life is suffering,
Every day a struggle,
Tormented from within and without
Compulsed to share visions
No one else can see,
To paint portraits of a turbulent world
Through the lens of a turbulent mind
On a luminescent night in Provence
Shimmering Venus and Ares framed
By the Asylum window,
An ecstatic celebration of life,
Ever moving; never resting,
Using pigments of agony, anguish and madness,
Transmuting lead into gold,
Depression into sunflowers,
Tragedy into beauty,
Brief breath of life into immortality.

3/30/17 (Vincent's 164th Birthday)

For Bob Dylan

Written on the occasion of Dylan being awarded the 2016 Nobel Prize for Literature.

Could be sung to the tune of "Song for Woody" by Bob Dylan, which was sung to the tune of "1913 Massacre" by Woody Guthrie.

You're out there traveling another mile down the road,
Listening for messages when the cold wind has blow'd,
Writin' 'em down and sendin' 'em out,
Trying to figure what this crazy world's all about.

Hey there, Bob Dylan, I wrote this for you,
'bout the songs that you write, the words ring so true,
Painting a picture of the world we both share,
Using vivid bright colors, write your poems in the air.

I see you sittin' out there on the Academy lawn,
Singin' Homer and Sappho from dusk til dawn,
With a voice as American as Whitman or Twain,
Wave as Jack and Allen, pass by on a hobo train.

Asking the questions no one else thought to ask,
Wearing grease paint on your Bob Dylan mask,
Singin' words shot straight through the soul
Travel in a caravan, hear the thunder roll.

I wonder did they ask, or give you a choice
Before declaring you their generations voice?
They pushed you on a pedestal so far in the sky,
You didn't sing while you slaved, they didn't care if you'd died.

A has-been they called you, washed-up and worse,
Others' expectations were your greatest curse,
Always changing, evolving; never the same,
They said that you'd lost, but you changed the whole game.

They say you came back, but you never left,
Singing songs made of history, love & theft,
The tour never ends, the show must go on,
Tempests may roar, the Titanic sails at dawn.

Thoughts, Dreams and Reflections
For Allen Ginsberg

I. Thoughts
I thought of you today, Allen Ginsberg,
As I often do when the howls from
Desolation Row enrapture my mind.
Rapid fired images stolen from
Dreams and nightmares of America.
Starving in the streets like
Hysterical angel headed hipsters
And raggedy vagabond doctors
Crouched in darkened doorways
Snarling, scratching at the
Constable's carriage for
A scrap of bread.

I saw you standing there, Allen Ginsberg,
In the alleyway behind Dylan.
Beautiful balding
Hippy bearded beatnik Buddha
Standing by with Aaron's staff
As Bobby chanted cue cards.
A roaring waterfall of words
Marching to an amphetamine driven
Breakneck Chuck Berry guitar beat,
Ducking down the alleyway looking
For a friend with a dollar to
Battle off the coon skin cap wearing
Cretin threatening to bust your balls
And break your thumbs.

II. Dreams

I dreamed of you tonight, Allen Ginsberg,
Walking in the California moonlight with a headache
Stopping by a San Francisco supermarket
To stalk the dream-ghost of Walt Whitman.
Peering through the produce of the all-night fruit stand
The peaches and plumbs ripe with juice,
You perceive, peripherally, a plethora of peasant people
Perusing the products at hand:

Mothers and fathers smuggling grapefruits
Inside pant-legs and purses
Sneaking out to feed frozen families.
Siddhartha and dear mother Eve
Discuss the nature of knowledge
While sampling the fig fruit on the aisle.
Woody Guthrie waiting by the watermelons
With Walt Whitman's niece, listening
As she reads from an old book of poems
Trying to remember the lines, memorize the rhymes
Tuning his laser guided six string fascist killer.

But amid the chaos of customers and cashiers,
Whose lines you never cross,
You never lose sight of your quarry,
That post Civil War Gandalf Greybeard
With his wide brimmed hat, piercing eyes
Staring out from under bushy old man eyebrows,
Face hidden beneath ancient Woden whiskers

III. Reflections

What will you talk about, Allen Ginsberg,
Later in your dream within my dream,
Walking arm and arm, no longer hunter and prey
Absently passing the canned pimentos and olive oil
As sunrise light breaks through
The five for a dollar avocado sign?
Will you walk out into the fresh dawn air,
Into the multicolored streets of the city
And speak of America?

America the beautiful ideal
Where elemental freedom burns
Thermonuclear fusion of love, liberty and equality
Glowing plasma at the heart of lady liberty's torch,
Shining out, warming and nurturing every inhabitant,
Free from birth to death, sons and daughters,
Grown and un-grown.
Land of the free, home of the brave,
Beacon of Justice throughout the world.

America, the schizophrenic reality.
Stealing land, slaughtering civilizations
Because Manifest Destiny.
America, home of upstanding brave patriot soldiers
ready to fight and wage war for freedom
To own human beings, buying & selling
Brown skinned children like cattle
Because Ham saw dear father Noah's dick
(Or whatever racist, revelation-based rationalization
Makes the biggest profit).

America that produced a captain like our Captain
To keep the ship from breaking up,
Steering her through stormy seas,
Brave defender of fragile so-called
Self-evident freedoms and truths:
If all men are equal; All men are free.
America that produced the man
Who shot our Captain in the back.

Will you take a stroll through Height Ashbury at dawn,
Or Morningside Heights in twilight?
Showing your friend around the campus of Columbia
The beautiful Butler Library,
Storehouse of knowledge and wisdom,
The spot where young Lou Gehrig
Hit a homer into the street.
Will you smile at the fresh-faced students
Studying physics and philosophy,
Sharing a smoke on the lawn,
Pack a picnic and dine in the shadow
Of Grant's tomb,
Pass a desolate tramp vomiting in the sewer
Near Nelson Rockefeller's portrait and
Speak of poetry and obscenity,
The sacred and the profane,
Art and pornography,
Literature and trash?

Who judges, how and why?
What phallic yardstick is it measured by?
What flow chart shows how to decide
The appropriate cock to verse ratio?
What recipe will tell how much "artistic value"
Must be added to write about double-D breasts

In iambic pentameter?
Is one asshole enough to get a book banned,
Or is it ass-fucking that tips us over the line?
Is missionary hetero-sex OK as long as
No one pisses on a crucifix,
Or do I need a different chart for that?

Where, where is the righteous moral outrage
For the truly obscene?

Censorship is obscene, banning books (Because you
Don't like it, nobody else can read it) is obscene,
Biased corporate owned media outlets
Filling empty headed TV and Internet hypnotized
Sheep brains with hate, fear and agendas is obscene
 A billionaire robber-baron with his hand
Shoved up a senator's anus is obscene,
Oligarchical plutocracy disguised as democracy is obscene
The destruction of the middle-class
And oppression of the working class is obscene,
Bigotry is obscene, homophobia is obscene, racism is obscene,
Denying people the right to marry
Because their skin pigment doesn't match--
Or because they genitals do-- is obscene,
Sexism is obscene, Antisemitism is obscene,
Justifying intolerant hate-think with
Religious proofs is obscene,
War is obscene,
Congressmen and businessmen wrapping themselves in the flag,
Sacrificing citizens and soldiers in Moloch's flames,
Worshiping the great Greenback God's golden calf is obscene,
Trading liberty for security (and getting neither) is obscene,
Push-button suicidal genocide that will
Burn the planet a dozen times over is obscene,

Mother's burying babies is obscene,
Mass-Murder in a kindergarten classroom is obscene!

Holy lotus blossom floating above
The sludge and sewage.
Lips cleansed, touched by a glowing coal,
Smoldering sacred stone,
Born by six-winged seraphim from God's
Smoke filled living-room hearth.
See, speak, sing the truth whispered in your ear:

Holy! Holy! Holy!
The whole world is holy,
The Universe is filled with glory!

Galaxies are holy! Constellations are holy!
Solar systems, stars and planets are holy!
Big Bang is holy! Black hole is holy!
Quark, atom and molecule is holy!
Life is holy! Evolution is holy!
Human, giraffe and dolphin is holy!
Male is holy! Female is holy!
Cock, vagina and asshole is holy!
Love is holy! Sex is holy!
Holding, caressing
Rubbing, spanking, whipping,
Exploding in ecstasy is holy!
The heart is holy! The brain is holy!
Reason, rationality and logic is holy!
Eliminating the impossible to
Deduce the Truth is holy!
The Truth, immutable, immaculate fact
Independent of opinion is holy!

Socrates is holy! Zeno is holy!
Chrysippus, Epictetus and Verissmus is holy!
Shit stained, urine soaked, whiskey scented
Homeless hobo is as holy as a
Purple robed, incense infused, bedazzled Pope.
Poets are holy! Prophets are holy!
Shamans, madmen and visionaries are holy!
Pens are holy! Keyboards are holy!
Canvas brushes, musical instruments and potter's wheels are holy!
The audience is holy! The performance is holy!
The stage, scenery and script is holy!
Sappho is holy! Catullus is holy!
Dante, Milton and Blake is holy!
Byron is holy! Keats is holy!
Verne, Wells and Shelley is holy!
Michelangelo is holy! Leonardo is holy!
Dali, van Gogh and Picasso is holy!
Muddy is holy! Woody is holy!
Robert Johnson, Elvis and Buddy Holly is holy!
Dylan is holy! LennonMcCartney is holy!
Townshend, Clapton and Hendrix is holy!
Lucky is holy! Lefty is holy!
Spike and Nelson Wilbury is holy!
Allen is holy! Jack is holy!
Neal, Burroughs and Whitman is holy!
The poem is holy! The word is holy!
John, Justine and Tristyn is holy!
Birth is holy! Death is holy!
Everyone and everything in between is holy!

Holy! Holy! Holy!

IV. Epilogue

Where are you now, Allen Ginsberg?
Out among the stars, sitting full lotus in the grass,
Meditating America?
Looking for a roundabout exit,
Sailing Samsara seas, searching a birth for your ship,
Walking the road from Rockland with Neal,
Singing songs of surreal Singapore sunlight,
Contemplating Eternity?

Are you with me here tonight, Allen Ginsberg,
Within the pages of your poems,
Bound up in the great book of breaths,
Inhaled through my brain,
Exhaled into the night?

Visions from the Wasteland

Standing alone in the wasteland
Of dying dreams and abandoned ideals,
I watched the greatest country in the world
Decay into an over-sexed, under-educated
Cesspool of self-gratification,
Intolerance and ignorance.

I saw culture, art, and creativity die,
Suffocated by the new plastic culture,
Whose sterile halls and prefabbed cathedrals
Were crowded with worshipers
Biting, kicking, scratching;
Trampling each other,
Screaming in a frenzy
Just to catch a glimpse
Of the great greenback god
And his hollow gifts,
Promising to fill the voids
And empty spaces
So you no longer wish to die.

I saw a once fit intelligent citizenry
Grow fat, lethargic, and dumb
Minds vegetating, souls atrophying
Entranced by hypnotic figures of light
Dancing in illuminated black boxes.

I saw an electric grid
Spread across the globe
Connecting distant countries
As next-door neighbors
While thickening the walls of our cells,

Isolated from the real touch of flesh,
Divided along the lines
They need us to fight,
Feeding us the truth
They need us to know,
Sucking the life from our veins.

I saw ignorance extolled as a virtue,
Confused with innocence,
Opinion and belief used to trump
Facts and Truth.
Facts manufactured and bred with
Fear and paranoia to suit the needs
Of oligarchical kings,
While anyone thinking outside the box
--outside their book--
Showing intelligence or critical thinking skills
Is ostracized; demonized
For not behaving like good little sheep.

Cries of oppression from those
No longer allowed to oppress,
Feeling persecuted because
Not everyone thinks as they do,
Feeling attacked because they can
No longer force lesser souls
To live by their rules.

I saw a people more offended
By peaceful nonviolent protests
Against injustice than by
Actual Nazis marching in the streets.

More concerned with who strangers
Love, fuck and marry than
Whether everyone has enough food to eat,
With making sure everyone shits
In their assigned areas than
Whether their neighbors
Get a death sentence
For being poor.

Master manipulator sleight of hand
Giving them something new and shiny
To be outraged about,
While they do as they please
Behind the curtain.

I saw superficial patriotism,
The last refuge of the scoundrel,
Worshiping symbols and songs,
Worried about winning and losing
Not about doing what's right.
Shallow worthless symbols
Bereft of the virtues that
Once stood behind them.

I saw a great nation,
One whole built from many,
Shattered, splintered, and schizophrenic,
Decadent, divided, and depraved,
Under the banner of big business,
The dry bones of the poor
Crushed to dust under the heels
Of profit driven privateers,
With liberty and justice for none.

Unfulfilled

40 years ago
16 flags unfurled o'er the fields
In the days after
The hard rain fell
And the thunder rolled.

Shepard and sheep
Soaked to the bone
Waiting for the warmth
Of the Sun to slide
Through dark clouds
And dry their wool.

Shuffling through the shadows
From the temple
To the marketplace
Without moving at all.

Merchants, thieves, and priests
Somehow sharing
The same space,
Thirsty for wealth, power, and praise.

Empty as a spent
Wine cask
That they desperately try
To refill with stale vinegar
Through cracked
Plastic straw.

Sing the Song of Rebellion

Singing the songs of my country,
Singing the songs of my land,
Serenading broken countrymen
Writing their dreams in the sand.

Telling the stories of our history,
All the lessons we should have learned:
The path that says it leads to greatness
Ends with human bodies being burned.

If you tell it often enough
Every lie can seem to be true,
The bigger the lie the better, it seems.
The great crowds won't have a clue.

Trained to reject the evidence of your eyes,
You'll see what they tell you to see,
Think what they tell you to think.
All the time believing you are free

This is how democracy ends:
With thunderous applause.
Sow the seeds of dissident rebellion,
Give voice to a sacred cause.

Golden Dreams

Dreams of cities paved in gold
--Gold, shiny glittering rocks
That people rape the Earth to obtain
And kill each other to keep--
Reality of soul sucked cities
Bathed in blood;
Washed in tears.

Miserable misers in golden towers,
Pay prostitutes to take golden showers.

While gold-less commoners
Scratch, scrape and struggle
For stale day-old bread,
Drenched in disease and despair
In the gutters and factories
Slaves to rent, groceries,
And rabid materialism.

Shiny black boot heels
Pressing down on their throats,
Finger pointing down the
Rat infested alleyway
Toward the new neighbors,
Whispers in desperate ears,
"Its their fault you can't stand up."

1984

Once they convince you
That the news is all fake,
That science is conspiracy,
To ignore the evidence of your eyes
--They're full of biased media lies--
That only they tell you Truth,
Alternative facts reversing the burden of proof,
Your best interests always in mind,

How do you prove
Climates are changing
In unnatural ways,
The past is immutable,
History is real, the Earth is old
Evolution is fact, Gravity works,
$2+2=4$?

How do you prove
That you're no longer free?

Shitholes and Assholes

Shitholes, assholes,
Misinformation, and lies.
Fascism, racism,
This is how democracy dies.

Demagogues, lapdogs,
Spineless senators falling in line.
Patriotism, nationalism,
White sheets at the scene of the crime.

Patriarchs, oligarchs,
Power, and greed,
Drawing strength from the blood
Of the poor on which they feed.

Imperialism, colonialism,
Conquest, and gain.
Materialism, Consumerism,
Neither will salve the existential pain.

Monarchy, anarchy,
Where does authority lie?
Dictators, traitors,
Watch democracy die.

America

Oh, America, you schizophrenic maladjusted
Nightmare train of well-intentioned paving stones,
What have we done now?

Feeling angry, frustrated and scared.
Things changing rapidly around you,
Up is down, black is white,
Majority today, minority tomorrow.
Afraid of being done unto as you have done.

Feeling dejected, ignored and disenfranchised,
By millionaire politicians that pretend to care about you
Every four to six years.

So, you shack up with the first sociopath that comes along,
Pays attention, tells you you're pretty,
And offers to take you away from it all.

Waking next day hungover regret,
Tiny hands cupping breasts under the sheets,
Spooning your ass, his limp little tool spent.
Just another trophy on a narcissist's wall.

America, Julia Roberts whore with a heart of gold
Waiting for the right billionaire to come along
And save you from the cold hard streets (and herpes).
Must've never read the Buddha's Dhammapada:
Nobody can Richard Gere you out of the whorehouse but you.

America, you under educated Ritalin starved paranoid
ADD suffering superstitious conspiracy theorist,
I love you, warts and all.

Despite oligarchy, plutocrats, and
Fucking the working class in the ass with the tax code.
Despite rampant racism, sexism, homophobia
And general xenophobic bigotry.
Despite egotism, corporate greed and the military industrial complex.
Despite manifest destiny and imperialist colonialism
Despite Corruption, Anti-intellectualism, elitism and hypocrisy.
I love you.
Not for what you are, or what you've been,
But what you dream of being:
Land of the free, Home of the brave,
Inalienable human rights to pursue
Life, liberty and happiness.
Equality and equity.
Sanctuary for huddled masses across the globe.

Once Upon a Time

Once upon a time
I saw you turn water into wine
The wine sat alone in the cellar
And no one has the guts to tell her
While wine gets better with age
She's just muddy vinegar at this stage

Watching the change to fascist regimes
Leonard Cohen haunts my walking dreams
The promise that Democracy will finally come
Orwellian nightmares causing my soul to numb
Though you've yet to be grabbed or kissed
Each of us have a duty to stand and resist

Should I even be here at my age,
Watching amateur actors prance on the stage?
What advice could I dare bequeath them,
A tip of the hat, a sad and sincere "Shalom aleikhem"
I could try and turn vinegar back into wine
Maybe it would have worked, once upon a time.

Time is Relative

The clock ticks
From morning til night.
One moment dawn light
Warms young faces,
Training wheels, and zoo trains.
The next, cold winter shadows
Fall and grow
Under the west setting sun.

Calendar pages fall away,
Torn, faded;
Yellowed by time,
Littering the ground
Like sun dried maple leaves
In October.

One by one,
Two by two,
Faces fade into twilight skies.
Passing away down trails
We cannot follow,
Until the day we do.

Not a Disney Princess
For Carrie Fisher

You took my breath away
All those years ago on the cinema screen,
A princess, but no damsel in distress,
Rescuing your rescuers;
Saving the day with a well-hidden blaster.
Leader, Warrior; Bad-Ass.

Out in the real world
Another sort of princess,
Born into Hollywood royalty,
But no less a hero,
Battling demons
From within and without,
Trapping them in books, screenplays and jokes,
Healing thyself,
Seeking a cure for the cures
With the shining sword of truth,
A beacon to the world,
Ashamed of nothing
Showing stigmatized, marginalized,
Demon haunted fans
To fear nothing as well,
And that—maybe
Demons are just learning-disabled angels after all.

You took my breath away
As you drowned in the moonlight
Strangled by your bra,
Your ashes wrapped in a giant
Prozac pill.
You can keep it, Princess

Gentle Breeze
For Glen Campbell

Counting the dirty cracks in the sidewalk,
Listening to a great old song,
Echoing through my ears,
Whispered on a warm summer breeze
From a southern night, long ago.
Memory's door is always open,
The path is free to tread:
A little boy singing with the radio,
Rhinestone dreams shared across the miles.
Bedrolls and sleeping bags,
Traveling down the line,
Spotlights and fan mail;
That subway token still inside my shoe.

The caress of your voice still lingers,
Transporting me across the miles,
Through the years,
And keeps you, forever, gentle on my mind.

There's a Dream I Keep Having
For Tom Petty (1950-2017)

A ten-year-old boy from Gainesville,
Whose uncle introduced his to Elvis
On a movie set in Ocala,
And traded his Wham-O® slingshot
For a stack of the King's 45s,
Saw the Beatles on Sullivan,
Bought a guitar, joined a band,
And never looked back
As he ran down that dream
Through the mud, across America
To L.A. for a date with Heartbreakers.

Damn the torpedoes, full speed ahead!
With his guitar, his band, and his southern accent.

Never giving in, never backing down,
Learning to fly with the stars;
Still singing with the voice of the people,
The voice of the poor,
The humble salt of the Earth,
The voice of the lonely,
The downtrodden, the unheard.

A rebel with a cause and a conscience,
Writing his truth,
Singing our lives,
Living his dream.

Your Last Secret
For Celine

Your dog was left in her living room,
Still on his leash.
This the only note you left,
The only sign that something
Was horribly wrong.

Alone you walked,
The salty breeze blown
From the Pacific.

How long did you sit
Listening to the rhythm of the waves—
Your thoughts totally and forever your own?
Your last secret,
Under the stars, among the waves.

Why? Why didn't you pick up the phone
Instead of picking up the gun?

The Last Supper is in Sight

I'm not ready for you to leave yet.
Though I know the time draws nearer
When you will excuse yourself from the table
And never come back.
Dinner only lasts so long;
Nobody stays forever.

When you got up to use the restroom,
I thought "This is what it will be like."
But I'm not ready for you to go.
There's so much more to talk about,
So many things I need to ask,
I need you to see who I've become
And be proud, as you always have been.

I'm not ready for this meal to end.
I'm not ready for you to go.

Answer the Call

Brush the moss off your shoulders,
Take flight, old nomad,
Though your feet have taken root.

They call to you,
And you must go.
They call you
Out of retirement from the road.
They need your help,
And you cannot refuse.
They call to you,
And you will go.

Hesitation, Self-doubt,
Its been so long, a lifetime ago.

Take up your staff,
Dust off your shoes.
They believe in you,
Even if you don't.
They need a hero,
To lead them from the darkness,
To navigate he wilderness,
To lead them home.
Take to the road
As if you never left it.

They call to you,
And you must answer.

The Night I Heard the News

For Karen S. Leys (1952-2018)

And then
You were gone.
A spark of anger
That I missed the chance
To see you one last time.
And then the reality...
Out into the night,
Cool air on my face,
Walking with no destination,
Thinking, processing the news.

Collapsing into the arms of family,
Gripped by seizures of grief.
You've gone
Where I cannot follow.
Gone, never to return.

They tell me you've gone
To a better place,
But what place could be better
Than one in which we're together?

Kaddish for Karen Leys (1952-2018)

Its so strange to think
That you're not there
In that little house on Salem Avenue
Sitting on the couch
Quietly reading fantasy novels on your Kindle
While Dad watches NCIS,
As if you'd always been there
And always would,
While I sit here across the mountains
Hunched over a notebook
Writing til my hand cramps
Trying to make sense of it all.

Less than a week ago
I stood before family, friend,
And virtual strangers
Eulogizing, reciting your life,
Explaining your souls,
Ukulele singing Over the Rainbow,
The Kaddish never too far away,
Drifting at the edge of consciousness,
Aramaic words and Hebrew letters,
Chanted, Sanctified
By deep Yiddish voices praising God.
But it never leaves my lips
--I can't remember the words,
The rhythm beating in my heart--
Besides, no one would understand,
Least of all me.

A week before,
Days after you'd passed,
Walking damp grass
Under a light rain,
Looking for my grandmother's grave
Near the lake.
Drawn to Hebrew engraved stones
Of no blood relation,
Rocks in hand to remember
Spiritual cousins,
Children of Abraham,
I breathe out Kaddish,
An involuntary response
Only the dead and I can hear.

Struggling, writing, composing for days
How to summarize a life, a soul
In words, pictures, and songs
--What my mother means to me
in 200 words or less--
Where to begin, what to say,
We all know how it ends.

Your parents' whirlwind wartime romance,
When peace came to the Pacific
Grandma brought his picture to the dock
To ensure she remembered his face.
A childhood with no fixed location,
Grandpa's restaurants, relocations, and wanderings.
Beatles and Meter-maids,
Rainbows and Munchkins,
Pretty little bluebirds fly,
Why, oh why, can't I?

Remember the Spring of '69
--Forever your favorite number--
When your eyes met his
For the very first time,
And your life changed forever.
A love born that would never die,
You never knew you could love
So completely.

Married a year later,
After missing Woodstock
Due to traffic.
Your father told you not to screw it up,
His father didn't bother to show up,
His mother, the hairdresser,
"Accidentally" turned your hair green,
But quickly remembered how to fix it
When she realized you weren't backing down.

The way he looked at you that day
--You can see it in the pictures--
You're his all, his everything,
Together you are finally whole.
When you died, we could all see
The empty space standing beside him.

Three years later
The picture what complete
As I entered ass-first
At the end of the Second Act,
Or was it the beginning of the Third?
Delivered by an Italian Catholic,
Circumcised by a New York Jew,
Named for two crazy uncles,

Two beloved brothers: John & Walter,
Christened in an Episcopal Church,
Cradled in Wally and Judy's arms,
The Godson who converted to Judaism,
And in whose heart the rhythm of the Kaddish beats.

You gave me life; you gave me everything.
You'd have given me the world,
If it was yours to give.
From New York to Oregon,
Baker City to Albany,
You created the perfect home,
Built of love, respect, and stability.

Toys and games,
Training wheels, roller skates,
And walks in the park.
Books and TV,
Whole universes inside my mind,
Narnia and Whoville,
Gotham City and Metropolis,
Strolling down to Sesame Street,
Across the trolley tracks from Mr. Roger's Neighborhood
Where the sidewalk ends in the Land of Make Believe.
Visiting Spiderman and Letterman at the Electric Company.
Playing with the Beaver and the Bradys
--Marcia was such a bitch--
Passengers on the Starship Enterprise,
Sailing away with Ramblin' Rod,
Choosing sides in a Family Feud
To decide if the Price is Right.
Going to war with Hogan's Heroes
And the Black Sheep Squadron,
Recovering at the 4077 M*A*S*H,

Back in time for Luke and Laura's wedding.

I went off to school,
But you were never far behind,
You spent so much time
Just waiting outside the school for me,
They invited you in
For PTA meetings, School Carnivals,
And volunteering in my class.

We moved once more,
Your last migration,
To that forever home on Salem Avenue
That you and Dad worked so hard to buy,
You lived and loved there 'til the day you died,
And I wouldn't have it any other way.

You gave me music,
Listening every morning
To the Country Western station:
Willie and Waylon,
Johnny and June,
Kenny Rogers as the Gambler.
You introduced me to The Beatles
Though a VHS copy of Help!
A gateway drug to Bob Dylan,
Changing my life forever.
I shared with you
My love of The Who
A new old group I discovered in '89.
Years later I'd take you to see them live,
Quadrophenia and Boris the Spider,
Pete, Roger, and John,
A memory I'll cherish forever.

You loved all children,
Not just your own,
--Though I know I was your favorite--
Worries for their safety
Made you a crossing guard at first,
And then—after being replaced by technology
A teacher's aide in the building where I went to school,
You'd attend there long after I'd moved on,
Educating, advocating,
Making them feel special and safe.
Greeting them every day at the door
With a smile to start their day,
Making sure they had breakfast
And school clothes,
Playing Santa and protector.

You mothered by friends
When you thought they needed it,
Last minute birthday parties
And Valentine chocolates,
Setting an example
Of what a parent should be.
Even into adulthood
To all my friends
You were Mom.

I went off to the Army,
But you were never far away,
Visiting me in Missouri
After basic training,
Christmas in Germany,
Dad's birthday at the Alamo.
Phone calls, letters, and vacations,

You were always with me,
And always will be.

After the Army I hit the open road,
Following my footsteps across America.
You supported every crazy scheme,
If you knew it was important to me.
From the gulf stream waters
Back to the New York Islands,
Knowing the road would always
Lead back to you.

You even accepted
And tried to understand
As I declared my soul Jewish,
Entering into the Covenant of Abraham,
Encountering the Kaddish for the first time.
You recalled with a smile
The kind Jewish pediatrician
Whispering in my ear,
Tallis draped across his shoulders,
Performing a Bris on a Gentile baby.

I returned for a while
To that comfortable cottage,
Sweetly situated on Salem Avenue,
But I was drawn away again
--Though not as far this time--
Across the mountains
By my all, my everything,
The love that made me whole.
And you understood
And were never far away.

You became a grandmother,
A role you were born for.
A new child to spoil and love,
And teach by your good example.
You loved him like blood,
And he loves you still,
Because love is not bound by DNA.

Baseball games and birthday parties,
Wedding dances over the rainbow,
Christmas and Hanukkah,
Packages of presents.
Lunch at Clear Lake,
Visiting Sahalie Falls,
Exploring the Secret Garden
At Belknap Hot springs.

Dad and you alone together,
Retiree road-trips just because you could.
Last minute trips to see the glaciers
Before they melt
And long planned vacations.
Short trips to the beach,
Red Wood trees and San Francisco trolleys.
You'd drive and hour
For the perfect piece of pie.

Day by day you grew sick and weak,
Your body turning against you,
But you never lost that spark,
Purple hair and teapots,
Tricked out walkers and wheelchairs,
You wouldn't be caught dead
With a boring cane.

You never cared what others thought,
You lived life your way,
And encouraged me to do the same.

I can still see the light in your eyes
When your grandson asked
To take you for a walk,
I'll forever remember the smile on your face
As he pushed your wheelchair
Down to Waverly Lake
One last time.

There was so much more
You wanted to see or do:
Celebrate 50 years with my father,
Watch your grandson graduate
High School and College,
And admire his firefighter uniform.
You'll be there for it all,
If only in our hearts.

Still at the podium,
Kaddish swaying in my brain,
A prayer for peace,
For shalom,
For wholeness and repair,

Trying to summarize
Your life and loves,
I conclude there
As I do here,
With the final words
Of the mystic Beatle
"Love One Another."

ACKNOWLEDGMENTS

The seeds of this book were planted when I wrote my first poem over thirty years ago. Since that time, I've learned and grown as a poet and as a person (and will hopefully continue to do so). Along the way there have been many people who have helped and encouraged me with regards to my poetry. A book's acknowledgements is a lot like an Academy Awards acceptance speech and I am sure that I will inadvertently leave somebody out. Just know that if you have supported my writing in any way, I truly appreciate it.

Thank you to

My parents, Tom and Karen Leys, both of whom are, sadly, no longer with us, having died within 11 months of each other between 2018 and 2019. They loved me unconditionally, they supported me no matter what, they were always proud, and always made sure I knew it. I literally wouldn't exist without them and definitely wouldn't be the person I am today without their example.

My wife, Justine, for all your support and encouragement. Part of the reason this book is being published now is because, after watching me procrastinate and continue to make up reasons why I needed to wait (the real reason being anxiety and insecurity), in June 2019 Justine gave me a deadline of 30 days to complete work on the manuscript and get it published. I wisely never asked what would happen if I missed the deadline!

My son, Tristyn, for all your support and enthusiasm when I've shown you things that I've written. I've always believed in you and it means a lot that you believe in me. Part of what drove me to finally publish this book was thinking how can I encourage you to follow your dreams if I don't follow my own?

My best friend, Tony III, for support, honest feedback, and always recognizing an obscure Dylan reference when you see it. Also, for helping me to see that being different isn't a bad thing

Kindra M. Austin, blogger, indie-poet, and novelist. An early fan and frequent commenter on my poetry blog. Your support, feedback, and encouragement have meant a lot. When I've needed a second opinion on something I've written, or needed self-publishing advice, you've always taken the time to answer my questions based on your own experiences and given me honest feedback. And thank you for your help in writing the book description for this collection.

Christine E. Ray, indie-poet, blogger, editor and creator of collectives. I can't thank you enough for inviting me to be a part of *Blood Into Ink*, including me in poetic collaborations, asking me to be a guest contributor to the *GoDogGo Café* blog, and generally making me feel a part of the online poetic community. Your inclusion of me in these many endeavors has done more for my self-esteem and confidence as a writer than I can easily express.

Sarah Doughty, indie author and poet, for asking the question that inspired 'How Does it Feel?'

All those who have read, and/or taken the time to comment on the poetry I have posted on my blog over the last three years. Your support, encouragement, and feedback were instrumental in my gaining enough confidence in my writing to actually publish a book. Your comments and positive responses to poems that I was sure nobody but myself would like have encouraged me to explore forms and topics I may have ignored or kept to myself thinking nobody would be interested.

ABOUT THE AUTHOR

John W. Leys is an indie-poet who been writing poetry since he was 14 years old, inspired by the words of John Lennon and Bob Dylan. His major poetic influences include Allen Ginsberg, Walt Whitman, Lord Byron, Erica Jong, Arthur Rimbaud, Sylvia Plath, Taliesin, the *Poetic Edda*, Catullus, Sappho, Ted Hughes, Leonard Cohen, George Harrison, John Milton, and Bob Dylan.

John was born on Long Island, New York and raised in Albany, Oregon. He served five years in the U.S. Army as a personnel clerk, received a Bachelor of Arts Degree in Religious Studies from the University of South Florida in Tampa and studied for his master's degree in Judaic Studies at the Graduate School of the Jewish Theological Seminary in New York City. He currently lives in Redmond, Oregon with his wife Justine, their son Tristyn, three dogs, and two cats.

He has had poetry published in *Omnibus*, the University of South Florida's literary journal, *Byronmania*, a now defunct on-line journal dedicated to Lord Byron, and Nicholas Gagnier's *All the Lonely People*. He has also contributed to a variety of poetry-blogs, including *Blood Into Ink, GoDogGo Café,* and *Free Verse Revolution*. His work can primarily be found on his own blog *Darkness of His Dreams*.

He is currently working on his second book, a collection of mythologically themed poetry.

Links
- Blog: darknessofhisdreams.wordpress.com/
- Facebook: facebook.com/darknessofhisdreams/
- Twitter: twitter.com/eliyahu5733
- Patreon: patreon.com/johnwleys

www.ingramcontent.com/pod-product-compliance
Lightning Source LLC
Chambersburg PA
CBHW060535030426
42337CB00021B/4272